GCSE Music Listening Tests

OCR

Ian Burton

R• RHINEGOLD EDUCATION

www.rhinegoldeducation.co.uk

Music Study Guides

GCSE, AS and A2 Music Study Guides (AQA, Edexcel and OCR)
GCSE, AS and A2 Music Listening Tests (AQA, Edexcel and OCR)
AS/A2 Music Technology Study Guide (Edexcel)
AS/A2 Music Technology Listening Tests (Edexcel)
Revision Guides for GCSE, AS and A2 Music (AQA, Edexcel and OCR)

Also available from Rhinegold Education

Key Stage 3 Listening Tests: Book 1 and Book 2
AS and A2 Music Harmony Workbooks
GCSE and AS Music Composition Workbooks
GCSE and AS Music Literacy Workbooks
Baroque Music in Focus, Film Music in Focus, Musicals in Focus
Music Technology from Scratch
Understanding Popular Music
Dictionary of Music in Sound

First published 2009 in Great Britain by
Rhinegold Education
14-15 Berners Street
London W1T 3LJ
www.rhinegoldeducation.co.uk

© Rhinegold Education
a division of Music Sales Limited

All rights reserved. No part of this publication may be reproduced, stored in a retrieval system, or transmitted in any form or by any means, electronic, mechanical, photocopying, recording or otherwise, without the prior permission of Rhinegold Education.

Rhinegold Education has used its best efforts in preparing this guide. It does not assume, and hereby disclaims, any liability to any party, for loss or damage caused by errors or omissions in the guide, whether such errors or omissions result from negligence, accident or other cause.

You should always check the current requirements of the examination, since these may change. Copies of the OCR specification can be downloaded from the OCR website at www.ocr.org.uk or may be purchased from OCR Publications, PO Box 5050, Annesley, Nottingham, NG15 0DL.
Telephone: 0870 770 6622   Email: publications@ocr.org.uk

OCR GCSE Music Listening Tests
Order No. RHG263
ISBN: 978-1-906178-92-5

Exclusive distributors:
Music Sales Limited
Distribution Centre, Newmarket Road
Bury St Edmunds, Suffolk IP33 3YB, UK

Printed in the EU

CONTENTS

INTRODUCTION	5
AREA OF STUDY 2: SHARED MUSIC	9
AREA OF STUDY 3: DANCE MUSIC	32
AREA OF STUDY 4: DESCRIPTIVE MUSIC	47
CROSS AREA OF STUDY QUESTIONS	68
GLOSSARY	73

THE AUTHOR

Ian Burton is Music Development Manager for Nottingham City Children's Services, where he runs the music service and led one of the three original pathfinders for Musical Futures. He has previously held posts in many areas of music education, including senior lecturer in music education at Huddersfield University, course leader for PGCE secondary-music at Bath Spa University College, and director of music in various comprehensive schools and an FE college. He has been principal examiner in composition for OCR A-level music, a subject adviser for AQA GCSE music, and was involved with the development of both A-level and GCSE music specifications. He is author of several of the earlier Rhinegold GCSE listening-test books, co-author of the Rhinegold AQA and OCR GCSE music study guides (first edition) and *Musical Futures: an approach to teaching and learning*, and a contributor to *Music Teacher* and *Classroom Music* magazines. He is active as a conductor, composer and arranger with a particular interest in creating opportunities for less experienced musicians.

ACKNOWLEDGEMENTS

The author would like to thank Abigail D'Amore for her invaluable help as consultant, and the Rhinegold editorial and design team of Harriet Power, Katherine Smith and Richard Gumbley for their expert support in the preparation of this book. Thanks too to Sarah Burton for her constant support and encouragement while writing this book, and to Carolyn Davis, Claire Dyer, Mike Gowland, Sarah Hant, and Helen and Rob Maddison for suggestions for tracks and for helping with checking the details of answers.

AUDIO TRACKS

Please note that there is no CD to accompany this book. All the tracks for these tests are available to download from iTunes.

Links to all the tracks can be found on the product page for this title on our website, www.rhinegoldeducation.co.uk.

TEACHER'S GUIDE

Answers to all of the questions and a full track listing are given in the accompanying *Teacher's Guide* (RHG264), available from Rhinegold Education.

INTRODUCTION

If you are reading this, the chances are that you're studying for GCSE music, using the OCR course (OCR is the name of the examination board). If so, congratulations, because you've chosen a good subject to study at GCSE, and one that's going to help you to get to know and really understand a wide range of music, some of which you may know already, but most of which you probably won't.

As part of your GCSE you have to take a listening examination: this lasts for up to 90 minutes and accounts for 25% of the marks for the entire GCSE. This book is designed to help you to do well in your listening exam.

WHAT YOU NEED TO KNOW FOR THE LISTENING EXAM: THE AREAS OF STUDY

> You can find more details about these Areas of Study in the specification that OCR publishes for GCSE music. Your teacher will have a copy of this, but you may like to look it up for yourself on the internet at www.ocr.org.uk/qualifications/type/gcse/amlw/music/index.aspx.
>
> The specification is almost 100 pages long, and most of it contains information for your teacher and school about how to actually run the GCSE course. However, section three of the specification is really helpful for you because it describes what you will need to know.

Because there is such a vast quantity of music in the world, including so many different musical styles, the OCR exam board has said that they will only ask questions about certain areas of music. These are called **Areas of Study**, and the ones that you will get questions about in the listening exam are:

- **Area of Study 2: Shared Music**. This is all about the ways musicians work together in a variety of different musical styles
- **Area of Study 3: Dance Music**. This is about the way music is designed for people to dance to in a whole range of different styles
- **Area of Study 4: Descriptive Music**. This is about the way music is used to tell a story, create a mood, or to act as the soundtrack to a film.

You may wonder what happened to Area of Study 1. This Area of Study is all about your own instrument, and because that could be different for every person taking the course, it doesn't feature in the listening exam.

You will notice that at the beginning of each listening test in this book you are told which Area of Study the test refers to. The Areas of Study contain a whole range of musical styles and key concepts. You should familiarise yourself with these styles and concepts as your exam will consist of questions based around them.

The table on the next page provides a brief summary of the Areas of Study.

Area of Study	Types of music to study	Key concepts
2: Shared Music	Romantic song Pop ballads The Classical concerto Jazz Indian classical music Gamelan Baroque and Classical chamber music The great choral classics African a cappella singing	1. How do musicians work together, and how are the relationships between musicians different across a variety of musical styles? For example, in different styles, who is in charge? ■ With a classical orchestra the conductor is totally in charge ■ In gamelan music the drum player controls the speed ■ In Romantic song the singer sets the speed, and often changes it – the piano accompanist has to follow every change. 2. How do performers learn pieces of music in different musical styles? ■ Some musicians learn from written music, while others learn by ear or by copying from CDs. Try asking musical friends and other members of your GCSE group how they learn to play pieces of music.
3: Dance Music	Waltz Tango Salsa American line dance Irish jig and reel Bhangra Disco Club dance	1. What features of the music are characteristic of each dance style? 2. What are the links between the music and the type of steps and moves made by the dancers? 3. Has music technology had an impact on the music?
4: Descriptive Music	Programme music (symphonic music from 1820 onwards) Film music	1. How have composers chosen and organised sounds to create moods, tell a story, set a scene or create dramatic impact? ■ A good way to prepare for this is to listen both to instrumental music that tells a story and to film soundtracks – in each case think about why particular musical features have been used for dramatic effect. 2. Has music technology had an impact on the music?
General	1. Know the names of some key performers and composers for each musical style. 2. Find out about the impact on the music of the type of place or occasion where that music is performed. What is its cultural background? ■ This sounds complicated but, for example, you will find that the musical differences between the two dance styles of waltz and bhangra are strongly related to their respective cultural backgrounds: the waltz from aristocratic ballrooms in 19th-century Vienna, and bhangra from Punjabi folk music and the club-dance scene.	

LANGUAGE FOR LEARNING

The language-for-learning list can be found in section three, part five of the OCR specification.

The exam board has produced a list called 'language for learning'. This is particularly helpful because it lists all the words and musical terms that you will need to know. You should try to understand what all these terms mean before taking your exam. The list can look long and a bit scary, but it is actually very helpful for you because it means that the exam board will only ask questions that use this musical language. There are various ways that you can get to know what all of these words mean:

- Your GCSE course is designed to help you to understand all of these features
- If you work through this book of listening tests you will come across most of the words and terms in the language-for-learning list. You will be able to actually hear what these words and musical terms describe
- The glossary at the back of this book explains many of the terms that you need to know
- You might want to get hold of the Rhinegold *OCR GCSE Music Study Guide*, as that goes into detail about all aspects of the GCSE course, including the musical language you need to know.

See www.rhinegold.co.uk for more on the OCR GCSE Music Study Guide (Rudland, Galley and Marshall, Rhinegold Education 2009).

USING THIS BOOK

As you work through the listening tests in this book, don't expect to get everything right first time. You can use this book as a series of mock exam papers, but it will probably be much more useful at first if you use each test as a tool to learn about a musical style.

You might find this a helpful way of working:

1. Read through the whole test carefully first. If there are any musical terms that you don't understand, ask your teacher to explain or demonstrate them, or look them up in the glossary at the back of this book.

2. Try using the correct number of playings listed at the top of each test. You will need to plan carefully what you are going to listen for with each playing, especially with the longer questions. If you don't think you can answer everything, then answer the bits that you can.

3. Some questions, particularly at the end of each test, are often more general (for example: 'What type of dance steps would you expect to see with this music?'). You can wait to answer these questions when the music has finished playing. Concentrate first on the ones where you really need to listen to the detail of the music.

4. When you've listened to the music for the correct number of playings, discuss with your teacher and the rest of your group any parts of the test that you had particular difficulty with. Listen to the music again and ask your teacher to help you to focus on these particular areas.

5. Look at the answers for each question (these can be found in the accompanying *Teacher's Guide*) and compare these with your own answers. With the more general questions, there are many potentially right answers, so don't panic if what you've written doesn't match up with the suggested answers – it might be that your answer is just as good.

6. If there are things that you got wrong, listen to the music again with the correct answers in front of you, and really try to understand why those answers are correct. If you're not sure, ask your teacher – you will learn far more by spending time going through each question in detail like this than by rapidly moving from one to the next.

FINALLY...

As you work through this book, you'll come across a range of music from a wide variety of musical styles. Some of them you may know, others may seem strange at first, but hopefully you will discover some new music that you really like. Whatever you think about any piece at first, concentrate on getting inside it and finding out how it works. These listening tests are designed to help you do this, and to discover the key features of each musical style. You'll probably find that the more you work at getting inside the music in this way, the more respect you will have for it, even for those pieces that you didn't like very much at first.

You should also find that by exploring all the different ways that musicians create music, it will give you ideas for your own compositions and help you to improve your own performances.

There is a whole world of music out there to explore, and this book is a small part of it. I hope you enjoy discovering the music covered here. Good luck with your musical exploration, and good luck with your exam.

AREA OF STUDY 2: SHARED MUSIC

TEST 1

You will hear **two** extracts of music from Area of Study 2: Shared Music. Both extracts come from a piano concerto by Beethoven.

Extract A followed by **extract B** will be played **three** times.

EXTRACT A

a. Underline the word that best describes the texture of the music:

  i. Played by the strings at the start of extract A.

  Heterophonic   Homophonic   Monophonic   Polyphonic

  ii. Played by the piano in extract A.

  Heterophonic   Homophonic   Monophonic   Polyphonic

b. Describe **two** other differences between the music played by the strings and that played by the piano in extract A.

  1. ....

  2. ....

c. Name the type of ornament heard in the piano part at the end of extract A.

  ....

EXTRACT B

d. How is the relationship between the piano and string instruments different in extract B?

  ....

  ....

  ....

  ....

  ....

TEST 2

This extract is based on Area of Study 2: Shared Music. A score of the first part of the extract is printed below. This extract will be played **four** times.

[Musical score in D major, 3/4 time, spanning bars 1–20, marked "Music continues..."]

a. Using the given rhythm, fill in the missing notes in bars 15 and 16.

b. Underline the word or phrase that describes the key the music has modulated to by bar 8.

    Dominant   Relative major   Relative minor   Subdominant

c. Underline the word that best describes the structure of the printed music.

    Binary   Rondo   Ternary   Variation

d. Describe **one** way in which the music is performed differently when each section is repeated.

....

e. On the score, draw a circle around **one** note that has been altered by an ornament.

AREA OF STUDY 2: SHARED MUSIC

f. This music features a continuo. What do you hear in the music that is characteristic of a continuo?

....

....

g. Describe what happens in the music when it continues after the end of the printed score.

....

....

h. Suggest a suitable composer for this music.

....

TEST 3

This extract is from Area of Study 2: Shared Music. You will hear this extract **four** times.

a. Underline the correct time signature for this music.

$\frac{3}{4}$ $\qquad$ $\frac{4}{4}$ $\qquad$ $\frac{6}{8}$ $\qquad$ $\frac{3}{2}$

b. i. Tick the box that best matches the sequence of chords heard at the start of this extract. Each box lasts for one bar.

| I⁷ | I⁷ | I⁷ | I⁷ | IV⁷ | IV⁷ | I⁷ | I⁷ | V⁷ | IV⁷ | I⁷ | I⁷ | ☐ |

| I⁷ | IV⁷ | I⁷ | I⁷ | IV⁷ | IV⁷ | IV⁷ | IV⁷ | I⁷ | I⁷ | I⁷ | I⁷ | ☐ |

| I⁷ | V⁷ | I⁷ | V⁷ | I⁷ | V⁷ | I⁷ | V⁷ | I⁷ | V⁷ | I⁷ | I⁷ | ☐ |

↑

> Not sure what these symbols mean? It may help to know that this piece is in B♭ major.
> - I⁷ means the tonic chord, with a seventh. In this key, that means B♭ major with a seventh (B♭–D–F–A♭)
> - IV⁷ means the subdominant chord, with a seventh. In this key, that means E♭ major with a seventh (E♭–G–B♭–D♭)
> - V⁷ means the dominant chord, with a seventh. In this key, that means F major with a seventh (F–A–C–E♭).

ii. What is the name for this kind of chord sequence?

....

AREA OF STUDY 2: SHARED MUSIC

c. i. Which instrument plays a solo in the second part of the extract?

....

ii. Complete the table to identify which **two** instruments accompany this solo, and describe the music that each instrument plays.

	Instrument accompanying the solo	Description of the music played by this instrument
1.		
2.		

d. This extract comes from near the beginning of the complete piece. From your knowledge of this type of music, describe what might happen next.

....

....

Performing idea

Try improvising a tune over the chord sequence heard in this extract, using a blues scale: B♭–D♭–E♭–E–F–A♭–B♭.

If you play a transposing instrument, such as clarinet, trumpet, saxophone or French horn, ask your teacher what the notes will be for your instrument.

TEST 4

You will hear **three** extracts of music from Area of Study 2: Shared Music. All three extracts are from a collection of songs by the same composer. The extracts will be played one after the other, **three** times – **extract A** followed by **extract B** followed by **extract C**, three times.

a. There are ten statements below. Each one applies to only one of the three extracts. In the boxes beside each statement, put the letter **A**, **B** or **C** to indicate to which extract each statement applies.

Features of the time/rhythm	
The music is in 6/8 time	☐
The music is in 4/4 time	☐
The music is in 3/8 time	☐
The performers make extensive use of rubato	☐
Features of the relationship between voice and piano	
The piano plays its own melody, quite different to the voice part	☐
The piano and the voice share the main melody	☐
The melody is in the voice part, and the piano plays repeated chords to support it	☐
Other features	
The extract is in strophic (verse) form	☐
The music starts in a minor key and modulates to a major key – it does this several times	☐
The vocal melody rises gradually over almost two octaves to build to a climax	☐

AREA OF STUDY 2: SHARED MUSIC

b. Underline the word that best describes the type of voice heard in these songs.

    Baritone   Soprano   Tenor   Treble

c. Suggest a suitable composer for these songs.

....

AREA OF STUDY 2: SHARED MUSIC   15

TEST 5

You will hear **one** extract of music from Area of Study 2: Shared Music. Listen to it **three** times.

This extract is an example of gamelan music.

a. Where in the world does this type of music originate from?

....

b. Identify **three** different types of instrument you can hear in this extract that are characteristic of gamelan music.

   1. ....

   2. ....

   3. ....

c. Apart from the instruments used, describe **four** other features that you can hear which are characteristic of gamelan music.

   1. ....

   2. ....

   3. ....

   4. ....

Exploring this music further

1. Watch different performances of this piece on YouTube (www.youtube.com): search for *Bubaran: Udan Mas*.

2. Although this type of music is normally learned by ear, you can find a notated version using numbers to represent the different notes of the scale at www.gamelan.org/library/notation/udanmasbonang.pdf. There is a simpler version, with just the core melody, at www.langensuka.asn.au/notation/Uler_Kambang_Udan_Mas.pdf. Note that these two versions use slightly different numberings (in the second version the 1's are replaced by 7's).

3. Try working out the core melody by ear and then devising your own performance using some of the techniques that you have described in your answer to question (c).

TEST 6

This extract is based on Area of Study 2: Shared Music. You will hear this extract **three** times.

a. This piece is an example of chamber music. What does this mean?

....

....

Finding it hard to distinguish them? Listen carefully at 8:23.

b. Identify the **four** instruments heard in this music.

1. .... 3. ....

2. .... 4. ....

c. What name is given to a group of four performers?

....

d. Describe **three** different ways that the four instruments relate to each other in this extract.

1. ....

2. ....

3. ....

e. Underline the type of cadence heard three times in the last few seconds of the extract.

      Imperfect   Interrupted   Perfect   Plagal

f. Suggest a suitable composer for this music.

....

AREA OF STUDY 2: SHARED MUSIC

TEST 7

You will hear **two** extracts of music from the same song, based on Area of Study 2: Shared Music.

EXTRACT A

Extract A is the first verse of the song, and is in the key of F major. In bars 13–17, three of the chords heard have been marked in boxes above the stave: chord I for the tonic chord of F major, chord VI for the relative minor chord of Dm and chord V for the dominant chord of C major.

Listen to extract A **four** times. The score on the next page is an approximate version of the sung melody.

a. Using the given rhythm, fill in the missing notes in bars 20–25.

b. In the empty boxes above bars 14 and 16:

    i. Write **IV** in one or more boxes where you hear the subdominant chord, B♭ major.

    ii. Write **V** in one or more boxes where you hear the dominant chord, C major.

Not sure about this? Read the words that are sung at that point.

c. Why do you think the composer has chosen these particular chords in bars 14–16?

....

d. Underline the word or phrase that best describes the accompaniment to extract A.

    Arpeggios   Block chords   Drone   12-bar blues

e. Underline the type of cadence that you hear in the last two bars of the printed music.

    Imperfect   Interrupted   Perfect   Plagal

AREA OF STUDY 2: SHARED MUSIC

3
I heard there was a sec - ret chord_ that
7
Dav - id played and it pleased the Lord, b'you don't real - ly care for mus - ic do yah?
12
I
VI
_ It goes like this, the fourth, the fifth, the mi - nor fall_ and the
16
V
ma - jor lift,_ the baf - fled king com - pos - ing Hal - le - lu - jah._
20
Ha - le - lu - jah. Ha - le - luh - jah. Hal - le -
25
lu - jah. Ha - le - lu_ jah.

Turn over

EXTRACT B

Now listen to extract B **two** times. Extract B is the last verse of the song.

f. Tick the box that best describes what happens to the key of the music in extract B.

☐ It is in the same key as extract A

☐ It modulates to a minor key

☐ It modulates to a key one tone higher than extract A

☐ It modulates to a key one tone lower than extract A

g. Describe **five** ways in which the music of the last verse (extract B) is more intense than in the first verse (extract A).

1. ....

2. ....

3. ....

4. ....

5. ....

TEST 8

This extract is from Area of Study 2: Shared Music. It is part of an Indian classical music performance. Listen to it **twice**.

> Not sure about this? Think about how the musicians will learn to play this music. Each musician will need to know how melody and rhythm are organised in this style of music. Think also about how the musicians will respond to each other during the performance. You might find it helpful to read pages 71–75 of the Rhinegold OCR GCSE Music Study Guide.

a. There are **three** different types of instrument heard in this extract. Complete the table below to describe the role that each instrument plays in the musical texture, and how each musician knows what notes or rhythm patterns to play.

Instrument	Role in the music?	How does the musician know what to play?
Sitar		
Tabla		
Tanpura		

b. Give the name of a musician who might be performing in this extract.

....

AREA OF STUDY 2: SHARED MUSIC

TEST 9

You will hear **one** extract of music from Area of Study 2: Shared Music. This extract will be played **three** times.

There are only three sets of words in this piece, although they are repeated:

Glory to God in the highest

And peace on earth

Goodwill towards men

a. Name the **four** types of voice that you hear in this extract.

1. .... 3. ....

2. .... 4. ....

b. There are several different musical textures in this extract. Using the table below, describe **two** features of the musical texture used for each set of words.

Words	Musical texture
Glory to God in the highest	1. 2.
And peace on earth	1. 2.
Goodwill towards men	1. 2.

AREA OF STUDY 2: SHARED MUSIC

> Word painting is where the composer uses music to illustrate the meaning of specific words.

c. Describe **two** ways in which the composer has made use of word painting in this extract.

1. ....

2. ....

d. In a large ensemble such as this, how do the performers keep in time?

....

e. Suggest a suitable composer for this music.

....

TEST 10

You will hear **two** extracts from Area of Study 2: Shared Music. They both come from the same track on the contemporary jazz album *Accident and Insurgency*. The track is about a fisherman living on a beach in East Anglia, who only goes out in really bad weather.

Extract A followed by **extract B** will be played **three** times.

EXTRACT A

a. Underline the most appropriate time signature for the first part of extract A.

$\frac{3}{4}$ $\frac{4}{4}$ $\frac{5}{4}$ $\frac{6}{8}$

b. Describe **two** features of the bass part when it plays near the beginning of extract A.

1. ....

2. ....

c. One of the performers on this recording is using a laptop computer. What sounds can you hear in extract A that rely on the use of music technology?

....

....

EXTRACT B

d. Identify the **two** different roles that the piano plays:

i. At the start of extract B.

....

ii. Near the end of extract B.

....

e. Underline the term that best describes what the bass plays throughout most of extract B.

   Drone   Ground bass   Riff   Walking bass

BOTH EXTRACTS

f. Compare the tempo of extract B with extract A.

....

....

g. Underline **three** features that you hear in these extracts.

   A cappella   Continuo   Improvisation

   Off-beat/syncopation   Scat   Son clave

   Swing rhythms   Round   12-bar blues

h. Extract A and extract B represent different sections in the structure of a typical jazz performance. How is the relationship between the performers different in extract A and extract B?

   i. Extract A ....

   ....

   ....

   ii. Extract B ....

   ....

   ....

i. How do you think the performers learned to play this music?

....

....

j. From your knowledge of jazz music, what might you expect to happen to end the whole piece?

....

AREA OF STUDY 2: SHARED MUSIC

TEST 11

You will hear **two** extracts of music, from the same song, that are based on Area of Study 2: Shared Music. Each extract will be played **three** times.

EXTRACT A

a. Give a suitable time signature for this music.

....

> Not sure what this means? If you had to play the chords in the introduction, how many different types of chords would you need to learn?

b. How many **different** chords do you hear before the voice comes in?

....

c. Tick the box that best describes how the different string instruments work together in this extract.

☐ They play a melody in unison

☐ They play a melody in octaves

☐ They play a melody at an interval of a 3rd apart

☐ They play a melody at an interval of a 7th apart

d. Describe **two** features of the relationship between the lead singer and the string instruments in this extract.

....

....

....

....

e. The extract ends with the words 'Looking like a beautiful day'. Describe **two** ways in which the vocal parts are different here compared to the rest of the extract.

1. ....

2. ....

AREA OF STUDY 2: SHARED MUSIC

EXTRACT B

f. **i.** Using the given rhythm, complete the pattern played by the strings throughout this extract.

ii. What is the technical name for a repeated pattern like this?

....

g. This extract consists of one musical phrase repeated over and over again: 'Throw those curtains wide, one day like this a year'd see me right'. Describe **four** features of the music that help to make it more intense as it builds up.

....

....

....

....

....

....

> **Composing idea**
>
> Use some of the techniques that you hear in this song to compose a piece of your own that gradually builds up and becomes more intense.

TEST 12

You will hear **two** extracts of music from Area of Study 2: Shared Music. **Extract A** followed by **extract B** will be played **two** times.

a. Underline the word or phrase that best describes the type of music heard:

    i. In extract A.

        Electro tango   Gamelan   Oratorio   Symphony

    ii. In extract B.

        Electro tango   Gamelan   Oratorio   Symphony

b. Underline the word or phrase that best describes the type of scale that the music is based on:

    i. In extract A.

        Blues   Major   Minor   Pélog

    ii. In extract B.

        Blues   Major   Minor   Pélog

c. Compare the context of these two extracts by completing the table below.

	Extract A	Extract B
How are the performers most likely to have learned the music?		
How do the performers stay in time together and know when to change tempo or dynamics?		
What sort of venue or environment is this music most likely to be performed in?		

AREA OF STUDY 2: SHARED MUSIC

TEST 13

You will hear **three** extracts of music from Area of Study 2: Shared Music. The extracts will be played one after the other, **three** times – **extract A** followed by **extract B** followed by **extract C**, three times.

a. The table below describes ten musical features. Each one applies to only one of the extracts. In the boxes beside each statement, put the letter **A**, **B** or **C** to indicate to which extract each statement applies.

Features of the instrumentation	
Strings, harpsichord, oboe and bassoon are heard	☐
Piano and string instruments are heard	☐
A continuo is heard	☐
Number of performers	
There are two performers	☐
There are four performers	☐
There are more than four performers	☐
Other features	
This is an example of lieder	☐
This is a concerto grosso	☐
The music is performed in strict time but with a ritenuto at the end	☐
Chromatic harmony is heard	☐

AREA OF STUDY 2: SHARED MUSIC

b. Each of these extracts is from a different period of musical history: Baroque, Classical and Romantic. For each extract, identify the correct period and give **one** musical reason for your choice.

	Period of musical history	Reason for your choice
Extract A		
Extract B		
Extract C		

AREA OF STUDY 3: DANCE MUSIC

TEST 14

You will hear an extract of bhangra music from Area of Study 3: Dance Music. This extract will be played **three** times.

a. Which two parts of the world have had the most influence on this musical style? Underline **two** answers.

  Africa   America   Argentina   Austria

  Britain   Cuba   Spain   Punjab

b. Describe **three** features of the music that are typical of bhangra.

  1. ....
  2. ....
  3. ....

c. Describe **four** ways in which music technology has been used in the creation of this music.

  1. ....
  2. ....
  3. ....
  4. ....

d. Where might you expect to see people dancing to this music?

  ....

TEST 15

This extract is based on Area of Study 3: Dance Music. The music is an Irish reel. You will hear this extract **three** times.

> Not sure about this? If you listen carefully, you'll hear that the music falls into four sections, each lasting about 7–8 seconds. Imagine representing each one of these sections by a letter – call the first one 'A' and then think about whether the other sections are the same (in which case call them A again), or different (in which case use a different letter).

a. **i.** Tick the box that best matches the structure of this extract.

☐ A B A B ☐ A B C D

☐ A A B B ☐ A A A B

ii. What is the name given to this type of musical structure?

....

b. **i.** Name the **two** instruments that play the melody.

1. ....

2. ....

ii. Tick the box that describes the interval between the two melody instruments.

☐ They play the tune in unison

☐ They play the tune in octaves

☐ They play the tune at the interval of a 3rd apart

☐ They play the tune at the interval of a 5th apart

iii. Name **one** other instrument that you can hear.

....

> You won't get marks for simply repeating musical features from earlier questions, so try to find other things that are characteristic of Irish reels.

c. Describe **three** other features that you hear which are characteristic of an Irish reel.

1. ....

2. ....

3. ....

AREA OF STUDY 3: DANCE MUSIC

TEST 16

You will hear **three** extracts of music from Area of Study 3: Dance Music. The extracts will be played one after the other, **two** times – **extract A** followed by **extract B** followed by **extract C**, two times.

a. The table below contains 11 musical features. For each feature tick **one** box to indicate which extract it is heard in.

	Extract A	Extract B	Extract C
Drum 'n' bass			
Trance			
Salsa			
The music is built entirely on a series of repeated loops, and panning is a major feature of the music			
Son clave			
Vocals have been overdubbed and treated with digital FX			
Vocals sung in Spanish – features a *pregón* and *choro*			
The only vocals are a sampled, whispered 'For an angel'			
Created entirely using music technology			
Performed live with no use of music technology			
Combines music technology with performers			

AREA OF STUDY 3: DANCE MUSIC

b. Which of these extracts is most likely to be danced in pairs?

   ....

c. Suggest a possible composer or performer for:

   i. Extract A ....

   ii. Extract B ....

   iii. Extract C ....

TEST 17

You will hear an extract of electro tango, based on Area of Study 3: Dance Music. You will hear this extract **three** times.

a. Complete the rhythm of the bass line heard throughout this extract:

b. After the bass line enters, how many **different** chords do you hear in this extract? Underline your answer.

One   Two   Three   Four

c. Describe **three** features of this music that are characteristic of tango.

1. ....

2. ....

3. ....

d. Describe **four** features of the music that have been created using music technology.

1. ....

2. ....

3. ....

4. ....

e. Give **two** reasons why this piece is suitable for dancing.

1. ....

2. ....

Composing idea

Try taking some of the key elements of tango and combining them with music technology. Use your answers to questions (c) and (d) as a starting point and then think how you might be able to achieve similar effects with the technology that you have available in school.

TEST 18

You will hear **two** extracts of music from Area of Study 3: Dance Music. **Extract A** followed by **extract B** will be played **three** times.

Compare the two extracts by completing the table below.

	Extract A	Extract B
Type of dance		
Time signature		
Harmony		
Instruments used		
Dance steps and movements used		

TEST 19

This extract is based on Area of Study 3: Dance Music. You will hear this extract **three** times.

This extract is an example of disco music.

a. Describe **four** features of this extract that are characteristic of disco.

1. ....

2. ....

3. ....

4. ....

b. Describe **three** features of the music that may have been created using music technology.

1. ....

2. ....

3. ....

c. Describe the dance steps and movements used in this type of dance.

....

....

d. Identify a suitable performer or group of performers for this music.

....

> **Extension idea**
>
> Listen to the whole of the track and try to map out the overall structure of the piece. See if you can identify a verse, chorus and middle-eight section. Are there any other sections? How has the composer put them all together? How does the song end?

TEST 20

You will hear **two** extracts of music from Area of Study 3: Dance Music. **Extract A** followed by **extract B** will be played **three** times.

a. The table below lists nine musical features. Beside each feature write **A**, **B** or **BOTH** to indicate if that feature is heard in extract A, extract B, or in both extracts.

Not sure about 3/2 time? This means there are two minim (rather than crotchet) beats to a bar. 3/2 is actually very similar to 3/4, but with more of a feel of two (rather than four) beats in a bar.

Time signature	
6/8 time	
3/2 time	
Type of dance	
Reel	
Jig	
Instruments	
Violin/fiddle	
Guitar	
Bodhran	
Other features	
Major key	
Binary form	

b. Both of these extracts contain complete melodies that are very short. How do musicians working in these musical styles usually turn these short melodies into longer dance pieces?

....

....

c. Underline **one** country in which the music from these extracts has its roots.

      Argentina   Austria   Cuba   Ireland

TEST 21

This extract is based on Area of Study 3: Dance Music. You will hear this extract **five** times.

a. Using the given rhythm, complete the melody in bars 8–13 **and** 21–25.

b. Tick **one** box to indicate the interval at which the printed melody line is doubled.

- [ ] Interval of a 2nd
- [ ] Interval of a 5th
- [ ] Interval of a 6th
- [ ] Interval of an octave

AREA OF STUDY 3: DANCE MUSIC

c. Describe the type of cadence heard in:

    i. Bars 14–15. ....

    ii. Bars 30–31. ....

d. Describe the music played by the harp.

....

e. What type of dance is this?

....

f. Describe **three** features of the music that are typical of this dance style.

    1. ....

    2. ....

    3. ....

g. Where did this type of music originate from?

....

h. Suggest a suitable composer for this music.

....

TEST 22

Extract A is from Area of Study 4: Descriptive Music. It comes from the film *Pirates of the Caribbean: the Curse of the Black Pearl*. **Extract B** is from Area of Study 3: Dance Music. It is a remix of the same piece of music.

Extract A followed by **extract B** will be played **three** times.

EXTRACT A

a. Tick the box for the rhythm played at the beginning of this extract.

b. Describe **three** features of the music that make it suitable for a pirate action film.

....

....

....

....

AREA OF STUDY 3: DANCE MUSIC

EXTRACT B

c. Describe **two** features of extract B that are characteristic of a remix.

....

....

....

d. Describe **four** ways in which music technology has been used to create this dance track.

....

....

....

....

....

....

....

TEST 23

This extract is from Area of Study 3: Dance Music. The extract will be played **three** times.

a. What type of dance is this?

   ....

b. Name **two** parts of the world where this type of music has its roots.

   1. ....

   2. ....

c. Underline the word or phrase that describes a type of rhythm **not** heard in this music.

    Cross rhythms   Polyrhythms

    Swing rhythms   Syncopated rhythms

d. Near the start of the extract, brass instruments play a repeated pattern several times.

   i. Underline the word that best describes this repeated pattern.

    Drone   Riff   Sequence   Scat

   ii. How many times is this pattern played? Underline your answer.

    Four   Six   Eight   Ten

   iii. Describe **two** ways that this pattern is different the last time it is played.

   1. ....

   2. ....

e. For each section of the band, describe what you hear that is characteristic of this musical style.

Vocals	
Piano	
Bass	
Brass	
Percussion	

TEST 24

This extract is based on Area of Study 3: Dance Music. You will hear this extract **three** times.

This extract is an example of tango.

a. Identify **three** instruments heard that are characteristic of tango.

1. ....

2. ....

3. ....

b. Describe **four** other features of the music that are characteristic of tango.

1. ....

2. ....

3. ....

4. ....

c. Describe the dance steps and movements used in this type of dance.

....

....

....

d. This extract is an example of a type of tango known as *tango nuevo*.

i. Describe **one** way in which tango nuevo is different to traditional tango.

....

ii. Suggest a suitable composer for this music.

....

AREA OF STUDY 4: DESCRIPTIVE MUSIC

TEST 25

You will hear **two** extracts of music from Area of Study 4: Descriptive Music. Both extracts are from a film called *The Bourne Supremacy*, and accompany a desperate foot chase through the streets of Berlin.

Extract A followed by **extract B** will be played **four** times.

EXTRACT A

a. i. Tick the box for the repeated melodic pattern that you hear at the start of extract A:

☐

☐

☐

☐

ii. Tick the box for the pitch at which this music is heard:

☐ Exactly at the written pitch

☐ One octave higher than written

☐ Two octaves higher than written

☐ One or more octaves lower than written

b. **i.** Which family of orchestral instruments is heard in extract A?

....

ii. Underline **two** words or phrases that describe features of the music played by these instruments.

Arpeggios	Glissando	Ostinato
Scat	Swing rhythms	Trills

> Not sure about this? A metronome mark of ♩ = 60 means there are 60 crotchet beats per minute – or each beat lasts for one second, which is quite slow. ♩ = 120 means 120 beats per minute, or two beats per second – fairly fast. Think these two tempos through in your head, then compare them with the speed of the beat in extract A.

c. Underline the metronome mark that best describes the tempo of extract A.

♩ = 40   ♩ = 80

♩ = 120   ♩ = 160

BOTH EXTRACTS

d. Compare the tempo of extract B with extract A.

....

e. Describe **four** ways in which the music of extract B creates a higher level of excitement and tension than in extract A.

1. ....

2. ....

3. ....

4. ....

f. Describe **two** features of the music that have been created using music technology. You may describe features of either or both extracts.

1. ....

2. ....

AREA OF STUDY 4: DESCRIPTIVE MUSIC

g. This film score is designed to match the action on the screen, and it combines music technology with live instruments. Describe briefly the process of creating and recording this music.

....

....

....

....

> **Composing idea**
>
> Try composing a piece of music for a tense chase scene, using some of the musical techniques heard in these extracts. Think about your answers to questions (e) and (f) then try to:
>
> - Combine a backing created through music technology with any live instruments in your GCSE group
> - Gradually build tension over the course of the music.
>
> Then think about your answer to question (g) and try to set up a session to record your music.

TEST 26

This extract is based on Area of Study 4: Descriptive Music. It comes from a film called *The Mummy: Tomb of the Dragon Emperor,* and aims to capture a spirit of adventure and excitement.

You will hear this extract **four** times.

Music continues...

Not sure what 1. and 2. mean in the music? The tune ends slightly differently the second time you hear it. The first time, you hear the music under the number 1 line. The second time, this bit is ignored and you go straight to the music under the number 2 line.

a. Using the given rhythm, fill in the missing notes in bars 17–19.

b. Identify **two** instruments or groups of instruments that play this tune.

   1. ....

   2. ....

c. The tonic chord (chord I) is heard in bars 12 and 13. On the score, circle **one** note that is harmonised with a dominant chord (chord V).

d. Describe **three** ways in which the composer has created a sense of adventure and excitement in this extract.

....

....

....

....

50   AREA OF STUDY 4: DESCRIPTIVE MUSIC

TEST 27

You will hear an extract of music from Area of Study 4: Descriptive Music. This extract will be played **three** times.

The music describes the true story of an expedition in 1912, led by the British explorer Robert Scott, who tried to be the first to get to the South Pole. His team did reach the pole, only to find that a team from Norway had beaten them to it. Struggling to return to civilisation, Scott's team ran into appalling weather conditions and were overcome by exhaustion, hunger and the extreme cold. They died, trapped in their tents by a blizzard, only 11 miles from safety…

Don't simply list things you hear – describe why each one is appropriate for the story.

→ Identify **six** features of the music that are appropriate for this story of a heroic struggle against nature in a bitterly cold landscape. You may refer to instruments, rhythm, melody, pitch, dynamics, texture or any other features that are relevant.

1. ....
   ....

2. ....
   ....

3. ....
   ....

4. ....
   ....

5. ....
   ....

6. ....
   ....

TEST 28

You will hear **one** extract of music from Area of Study 4: Descriptive Music. The extract will be played **four** times.

This extract comes from a piece called *Danse Macabre*, which tells a tale of how, at midnight on Halloween, in a deserted cemetery, Death appears and starts playing the violin; skeletons come out of their graves and begin to dance to the music...

a. Using the given rhythm, fill in the missing notes in the melody played by the violin at the beginning of the extract.

b. This melody is heard again later in the extract. Describe **two** ways in which it is performed differently the second time.

1. ....

2. ....

Not sure where this is? Listen carefully at 1:43.

c. Name the percussion instrument that plays a melody later on in the extract.

....

52 AREA OF STUDY 4: DESCRIPTIVE MUSIC

> Not sure where this is? Listen to the extract from 1:56 to 2:25.

d. Underline **three** words or statements that describe musical features you can hear in the last part of the extract.

    A cappella   Cadenza   Counterpoint

    Fugue   Glissando   Middle eight

    Retrograde motion   Rubato   Swing rhythms

    A variation on a melody heard earlier

> Don't simply list things you hear – describe why each feature helps to create an approriate atmosphere.

e. Describe **three** features of the music that help to create an appropriate atmosphere for the story.

....

....

....

....

....

AREA OF STUDY 4: DESCRIPTIVE MUSIC

TEST 29

You will hear **three** extracts of music from a film called *Hellboy*. The extracts relate to Area of Study 4: Descriptive Music.

Hellboy is a strange superhero. Seven-foot tall, bright red, with a tail and a stone fist, he looks pretty scary, but he has a definite sense of style and spends his life protecting the world from evil. He also has a well-hidden gentler side: he likes kittens and genuinely cares for Liz, his girlfriend.

These extracts show different sides of Hellboy's character.

Extract A followed by **extract B** will be played **three** times.

EXTRACT A

a. i. Using the given pitches, write out the main theme, first heard a few seconds into the track.

This is Hellboy's main leitmotif – a theme that represents a character throughout a film. The composer will vary the tune to reflect the dramatic situation. To find out more, read pages 146–153 in the Rhinegold OCR GCSE Music Study Guide.

ii. What is the technical term used when a tune starts on the last beat of a bar?

....

EXTRACT B

b. i. Underline the word that best describes the tempo of this extract.

        Allegro   Largo   Moderato   Presto

54   AREA OF STUDY 4: DESCRIPTIVE MUSIC

ii. Underline the word that best describes the type of harmony heard in this extract.

    Atonal   Chromatic   Diatonic   Dissonant

iii. What is unusual about the harmony at the very end of the extract?

....

> In this type of question, you won't get many marks just for listing instruments or musical features – you need to show how those features help to create the different sides of Hellboy's character.

COMPARISON OF EXTRACTS A AND B

c. Use the headings in the table below to compare the music for extracts A and B. Describe how elements of the music bring out the different sides of Hellboy's character.

	Extract A (main Hellboy theme)	Extract B (main love theme: Hellboy and Liz)
Use of tempo and rhythm		
Use of melody and harmony		
Use of instruments		

AREA OF STUDY 4: DESCRIPTIVE MUSIC

COMPARISON OF EXTRACTS A AND C

You will now hear **extract A** followed by **extract C two** times.

Extract C comes from the end of the film, when Hellboy fights heroically to finally conquer the forces of evil.

> You will probably spot the use of the main Hellboy theme near the start, but also listen carefully at 2:12–2:22.

d. Describe **two** ways in which the main Hellboy theme (from extract A) is heard differently in extract C.

....

....

....

....

TEST 30

You will hear **two** extracts of music from Area of Study 4: Descriptive Music. This music was written for a film, set in World War II, in which a group of British soldiers parachute into Germany on an 'impossible' mission to try to rescue an American general who holds all the secret plans for D-Day. However, there is at least one traitor on the British team, and when they do rescue the general they find that the situation is far more complex than they thought, and nobody is who they seem to be...

Extract A followed by **extract B** will be played **four** times.

EXTRACT A

a. i. Identify the instrument that plays at the beginning of extract A.

....

The rhythm pattern is played three times before any other instruments come in.

ii. Which of the following patterns is correct for the rhythm played by this instrument at the start of the extract? Tick the box next to your chosen answer.

AREA OF STUDY 4: DESCRIPTIVE MUSIC

EXTRACT B

b. i. Identify the family of instruments that play at the start of extract B.

....

ii. Underline the word that best describes the structure of the music in the first half of the extract.

    Fugue   Rondo   Strophic   Ternary

BOTH EXTRACTS

Give a suitable dynamic marking for:

c. i. The start of extract A. ....

  ii. The end of extract B. ....

d. i. Tick **one** box to show how the music modulates in extract A.

☐ Stays in the same key and does not modulate

☐ Starts in a minor key, modulates through several different keys and ends in a minor key

☐ Starts in a minor key, modulates through several different keys and ends in a major key

☐ Starts in a major key and modulates to the relative minor

  ii. Tick **one** box to show how the music modulates in extract B.

☐ Stays in the same key and does not modulate

☐ Starts in a minor key, modulates through several different keys and ends in a minor key

☐ Starts in a minor key, modulates through several different keys and ends in a major key

☐ Starts in a major key and modulates to the relative minor

e. Describe **four** features of the music from either or both extracts that help to capture the right mood for the story.

....

....

....

....

....

....

....

f. Describe **one** similarity and **one** difference between extract A and extract B.

Similarity:

....

Difference:

....

AREA OF STUDY 4: DESCRIPTIVE MUSIC

TEST 31

You will hear **three** extracts of music from Area of Study 4: Descriptive Music. They come from the film *Superman*.

The extracts will be played one after the other, **three** times – **extract A** followed by **extract B** followed by **extract C**, three times.

a. Nine musical features are described in the table below. Tick **one** box for each feature to show which extract it is heard in.

	Extract A	Extract B	Extract C
Diatonic melody and harmony, stays in same key throughout			
Mainly diatonic melody and harmony, changes key for different sections			
Chromatic melody and harmony, keeps making odd jumps to different keys			
Tune played by brass, accompanied by this rhythm heard over and over again:			
Main tune played largely by woodwind instruments and tuba			
The flow of the music is interrupted several times by snarling sounds on brass instruments			
A slow, gradual crescendo			
Compound time signature			
Canon and imitation			

AREA OF STUDY 4: DESCRIPTIVE MUSIC

b. These extracts represent three of the key characters and places in the film. Complete the table below to identify which extract relates to each character or place, and describe **two** features of each extract that help to portray that character or place.

Character/place	Which extract?	Features of the music that make it dramatically effective
Superman, faster than a speeding bullet, able to fly, a symbol of hope		1. 2.
The villain Lex Luthor and his rather incompetent assistants		1. 2.
The majestic main city on the planet Krypton		1. 2.

AREA OF STUDY 4: DESCRIPTIVE MUSIC

TEST 32

This extract is based on Area of Study 4: Descriptive Music. The music describes how the hero sneaks into the lair of the Mountain King and then desperately tries to escape, pursued by trolls and the Mountain King himself!

You will hear this extract **three** times.

a. Which of the following note patterns is the correct shape for the melody **at the beginning** of this extract? Tick the box next to your chosen answer.

b. Underline the word that describes how the string instruments are played in the first part of the piece.

        Arco   Legato   Pizzicato   Tremolo

AREA OF STUDY 4: DESCRIPTIVE MUSIC

c. Using the following headings, explain how the music creates a sense of increasing excitement and panic.

Tempo of the music	
Use of pitch	
Use of dynamics	
The way the instruments are used	

d. Suggest a suitable composer for this music.

....

AREA OF STUDY 4: DESCRIPTIVE MUSIC

TEST 33

You will hear **one** extract of music from Area of Study 4: Descriptive Music. This music is from the beginning of a James Bond film. The action of this section of the film (together with approximate timings) is given in the grid below.

0:00	An American space capsule is orbiting the Earth, floating in the depths of space
0:23	One of two astronauts opens the capsule hatch and goes out for a space walk, still attached to the capsule via a lifeline
1:04	The radar picks up an unidentified spacecraft, closing fast on the American capsule. The astronauts see a large spacecraft heading directly for them
1:43	The shark-like front of the enemy craft starts to open
2:01	The jaws of the enemy craft slowly close over the American capsule so as to completely swallow it
2:19	The jaws of the enemy craft slam shut and, in doing so, snap the lifeline of the space-walking astronaut, who floats off helplessly into the emptiness of space

This extract will be played **three** times.

a. Underline the word or phrase that describes the musical device heard in the extract.

      Fugue   Ostinato   Retrograde motion   Walking bass

b. Describe **four** ways in which the music creates an appropriate atmosphere for the depths of space.

....

....

....

....

....

c. Describe **four** ways in which the music creates an increasing sense of tension.

....

....

AREA OF STUDY 4: DESCRIPTIVE MUSIC

....

....

....

....

d. Suggest a suitable composer for this music.

....

> **Performing idea**
>
> Try performing or sequencing this music yourself, using this simplified score as a starting point:
>
> ■ This four-bar sequence repeats over and over again, starting with a single line and gradually adding the other parts at key moments in the drama
> ■ The suggested instruments can be replaced by any available acoustic or synthesised alternatives
> ■ The keyboard part can be split between two hands (with the left hand taking the first two notes of the first three bars), or could be played at half speed (crotchet triplets) to make a simpler version. If possible a sustaining pedal should be used to blur the sound in each bar
> ■ If desired, the coda/climax of the original score can be recreated by holding a (tremolo) G minor chord and repeating the first two bars of the trumpet part four times.

AREA OF STUDY 4: DESCRIPTIVE MUSIC

TEST 34

This extract is based on Area of Study 4: Descriptive Music. The music is intended to portray a gnome – a strange, menacing creature. You will hear this extract **three** times.

a. Tick the box that describes the harmony in this extract.

☐ Major key, diatonic harmony

☐ Minor key, diatonic harmony

☐ Minor key, chromatic harmony

☐ Atonal harmony

b. Using the following headings, describe how the music creates a feeling of strangeness and menace. You should aim to make **two** points under each heading.

The tempo of the music	
The use of dynamics	
The way that the instruments are used	

AREA OF STUDY 4: DESCRIPTIVE MUSIC

> Not sure about this? Listen carefully to what happens after the final chord of the extract.

c. **i.** What feature of the actual recording adds to the feeling of strangeness?

....

ii. How might this effect have been achieved?

....

> **Composing idea**
>
> Compose a piece of music that portrays a fantasy character (perhaps one of the characters from the Harry Potter books).
>
> Whichever character you pick, think about what that character is like, and what musical features you could use to represent them. For example:
>
> - Is the character warm and friendly, or slimy and scary?
> - How heavy is your character?
> - How does the character move – very slowly? Very fast? With sudden changes of direction?
> - What mood is your character in? Happy? Angry? Sad? In love? Constipated?

CROSS AREA OF STUDY QUESTIONS

TEST 35

You will hear **three** extracts of music, one each from Areas of Study 2, 3 and 4. Each extract will be played **three** times.

EXTRACT A

This extract is based on Area of Study 3: Dance Music. You will hear this extract **three** times.

a. What type of dance is this?

....

b. Tick the box that best describes the order that the instruments and voices enter in this extract.

Brass	Lead singer	Bass, congas and timbales	Shouts and claps	Backing vocals	Piano and guiro	☐
Shouts and claps	Piano and guiro	Bass, congas and timbales	Brass	Backing vocals	Lead singer	☐
Shouts and claps	Bass, congas and timbales	Piano and guiro	Brass	Lead singer	Backing vocals	☐
Shouts and claps	Piano and guiro	Brass	Backing vocals	Bass, congas and timbales	Lead singer	☐

c. Describe the dance steps and movements used in this type of dance.

....

....

....

EXTRACT B

This extract is based on Area of Study 4: Descriptive Music. You will hear this extract **three** times.

It describes an artist being carried, as part of a marching procession, to a guillotine, where he is to be beheaded. At the last minute, just before the blade comes down, he thinks of the girl he loves ... The guillotine descends and the crowd cheers (because they think it's great public entertainment)...

d. Complete the table below to show how the composer uses music to portray each section of the story.

Section of the story	How the music portrays the story
Prisoner carried in a marching procession up to the guillotine	
The crowd goes silent, he thinks for one last time of the one he loves ... The guillotine comes down and beheads him	
The crowd rejoices	

EXTRACT C

This extract is based on Area of Study 2: Shared Music. You will hear this extract **three** times.

e. Underline the country that this music originates from.

      Africa   America   Cuba   India

f. Identify **three** instruments heard in this extract.

1. ....

2. ....

3. ....

g. Underline the musical feature you can hear in this extract.

      Drone   Ground bass   Modulation   Walking bass

ALL EXTRACTS

Now think about all three of the extracts.

h. Write **A**, **B** or **C** in the box beside each statement to show which extract it refers to.

- ☐ The musicians will have learned this music from written music notation
- ☐ The musicians are improvising with raga and tala patterns
- ☐ The musicians will have learned the repeated patterns by ear, with some improvisation from soloists in call-and-response sections

TEST 36

You will hear **three** extracts of music, one each from Areas of Study 2, 3 and 4. Each extract will be played **twice**.

EXTRACT A

This extract is based on Area of Study 2: Shared Music. You will hear this extract **twice**.

a. Underline **three** words or phrases that describe features heard in this extract.

A cappella	Atonal harmony	Call and response
Chromatic harmony	Counterpoint	Heterophony
Male voices	Mixed male and female voices	Swing rhythms

b. i. How does the tempo change in this extract?

....

ii. How do the musicians keep together during the tempo change(s)?

....

c. Which part of the world does this music originate from?

....

EXTRACT B

This extract is based on Area of Study 4: Descriptive Music. It is from a piece of music that depicts skeletons, having risen from their graves, taking part in an increasingly wild dance of death – only to be cut short by the arrival of dawn.

You will hear this extract **twice**.

CROSS AREA OF STUDY QUESTIONS

d. Describe **three** ways in which the composer has represented the story in his music.

....

....

....

....

....

e. i. How does the tempo change in this extract?

....

ii. How do the musicians keep together during the tempo change(s)?

....

EXTRACT C

This extract is based on Area of Study 3: Dance Music. It is a remix, in a trance style, of music from the film *Pirates of the Caribbean: the Curse of the Black Pearl*. You will hear this extract **twice**.

f. Describe **three** features of this extract that are characteristic of club-dance music.

....

....

....

....

....

g. In extracts A and B, the musicians creating the performance had to work together to cope with changes in tempo. Give **two** reasons why this is not a problem in extract C.

1. ....

2. ....

CROSS AREA OF STUDY QUESTIONS

GLOSSARY

A cappella. Refers to unaccompanied ensemble singing of any genre.

Accent. Emphasis on a note or chord. Sometimes indicated by the symbol >.

Accompaniment. Music that supports a main performer or melody. For example, a pianist might accompany a solo instrumentalist or singer, supplying harmony to support the melodic line.

Acoustic. A version of an instrument that does not have any form of electronic amplification built in.

Allegro. Italian for 'cheerful'. A quick tempo marking.

Alto. A low female voice.

Anacrusis. An upbeat. A note or group of notes that come before the first strong beat of a phrase.

Andante. Italian for 'walking'. A medium tempo marking.

Arco. A direction to bow notes on a string instrument.

Arpeggio. A chord in which the notes are played one after the other rather than at the same time. For example, an arpeggio of the chord F major could be played as F, A, C, F.

Atonal. Western music that wholly or largely does not use keys or modes.

Aural. To do with listening; refers to using the ear to hear, rather than the mouth to speak.

Backing vocals/singers. A group of singers in a band who support the main vocalist(s), by singing harmony in the background of a song.

Bandoneón. An accordion used in tango music.

Baritone. A male voice that lies between tenor and bass.

Baroque. The period of music between 1600 and 1750.

Bass line. The lowest-pitched line in a piece of music, on which the harmonies are based.

Bass singer. The lowest male voice.

Beats per minute. Indicates the tempo of a piece by specifying how many beats there should be each minute. *See* **Metronome mark**.

Bhangra. A type of dance that originated in the Punjab region of north India and Pakistan. Traditional bhangra fused with western popular music in the UK during the 1970s and 80s.

Binary form. A musical structure of two sections with contrasting material in each (AB).

Block chord. A chord in which the notes are played together at the same time.

Blues scale. A scale often used in jazz and blues music, useful for improvising over twelve-bar blues chord patterns. Compared to a normal major scale, it features a flattened third, fifth and seventh, with a normal (perfect) fourth and fifth: if starting on C, the scale would be C, E♭, F, G♭, G, B♭, C.

Bodhran. An Irish frame drum.

Broken chord. *See* **Arpeggio**.

Cadence. Formed by the last two chords of a phrase, a type of musical punctuation. *See* **Imperfect cadence**, **Interrupted cadence**, **Perfect cadence** and **Plagal cadence**.

Cadenza. An unaccompanied showpiece for the soloist in a concerto.

Call and response. A pair of phrases, usually performed by different musicians, in which the second phrase is heard as a reply to the first. This term normally refers to jazz and pop music. Similar to **question and answer**.

Canon. A musical structure in which the melody in one part is repeated exactly by the other parts, while the original part continues with different music.

Chaal rhythm. A repeated eight-note pattern played by the dhol in bhangra music:

Chamber music. A genre of music for small groups of musicians, such as a string quartet, in which each musician plays an individual part.

Chord sequence. A series of chords. The twelve-bar blues is one example of a well-known chord sequence.

Chorus. In popular music, this refers to the repeated refrain in a verse-and-chorus structure.

Chromatic. Refers to notes that do not belong to the scale of the key that the music is currently in. For example, B♮ and D♯ are chromatic notes in the key of F major.

Classical. The period of music between 1750 and 1830.

Click track. A track with a basic, steady click rhythm used to provide a beat for musicians to play along to.

Close harmony. When the notes of each chord are not spaced out but are close together in range.

Comping. In jazz music, an improvised style of piano playing that accompanies the solo lines.

Compound time. A metre in which the main beat is subdivided into three equal portions.

Concerto. A piece of music for an instrumental soloist and orchestra, often in three movements.

Concerto grosso. A type of music developed in the Baroque era using two distinct groups of instruments: a small group (the concertino) and a full orchestra (the ripieno).

Conductor. The leader of a choir or orchestra, who stands out in front of the singers and players to direct them.

Congas. A pair of tall, narrow, single-headed drums. Congas originated in Cuba and are played in popular styles such as salsa.

Continuo. An accompanying part in instrumental music of the Baroque period. The continuo is played by a bass instrument (such as cello) and a harmony instrument (such as harpsichord).

Contrapuntal. A texture in which two or more melodic lines, each one significant in itself, are played together at the same time.

Countermelody. A second melody in a piece that is heard at the same time as the main melody, to provide a contrast.

Counterpoint. *See* **Contrapuntal**.

Crescendo. Gradually get louder. Opposite of **decrescendo**.

Cross rhythm. A rhythm that conflicts with the regular pattern of stressed and unstressed beats in a piece of music, or the combination of two conflicting rhythms within a single beat (e.g. duplets against triplets).

Cycle. A melodic, rhythmic or harmonic pattern, or a section of music, that is repeated a number of times.

Decrescendo. Gradually get quieter. Opposite of **crescendo**.

Delay. An audio effect that can be electronically added to music to give the effect of an echo.

Dhol. A double-headed drum held with a strap around the player's neck, used in bhangra music.

Diatonic. Music containing notes that belong to the scale of the key that the music is currently in. For example, B♭ and D are diatonic notes in the key of F major.

Digital effects. Processes applied to a signal to alter its sound quality in some way, or the devices used to do so.

Diminuendo. *See* **Decrescendo**.

Disco. A type of popular dance developed in the 1960s and 70s in New York discotheques.

Dissonant. A combination of notes that produces a clashing sound when played together.

Distortion. An effect that alters a music signal to add overtones, giving the sound a richer or more aggressive feel.

Dominant. The fifth note of a scale. For example, C is the dominant of F.

Dotted rhythms. A dot placed immediately after a note increases its value by half. For example, a dotted minim lasts for three crotchet beats (two crotchets for the minim plus one for the dot).

Drone. A sustained note that is held in one part while other parts play or sing melodies against it.

Drum machine. An electronic device that replicates the sounds of various percussion instruments.

Drum 'n' bass. A genre of electronic dance music that developed in the 1990s.

Dynamics. How loudly or softly the music is played; the volume of the music. Indicated by dynamic markings such as piano (quiet) and crescendo (gradually get louder).

Echo. An effect that repeats a sound at regular intervals more softly each time.

Electro tango. A sub-genre of tango that incorporates electronic music and digital effects.

Ensemble. A group of musicians performing together.

Forte/fortissimo. A dynamic marking: loud/very loud.

Fugue. A musical form in which a main theme is taken up and developed by each of the parts in turn.

FX. *See* **Digital effects**.

FX pedal. A piece of electronic musical equipment used to add one or several effects (distortion, echo, etc.) to an instrument.

Gamelan. An ensemble of tuned percussion instruments from Indonesia.

Glissando. A slide from one pitch to another.

Ground bass. A structural device involving a phrase in the bass that is repeated throughout the piece.

Guiro. A percussion instrument made from a gourd which is scraped with a stick. Used in Latin-American music.

Harmony. The combination of chords used in a piece of music. To study harmony we look at the vertical aspects of the music (the chords, and how they change) instead of the horizontal aspects (the melody, and how it evolves).

Harmonic rhythm. How often the harmony changes in a passage of music.

Harp. A plucked string instrument.

Head. The main theme in a jazz piece.

Heterophonic/heterophony. A texture in which different versions of the same melody are heard simultaneously.

Hi-hat. Two cymbals on a stand that open and close; found in a typical drum kit.

Homophonic. A texture in which all parts (melody and accompaniment) move with a similar/the same rhythm, creating a chordal effect.

Imitation. A melodic idea in one part is immediately copied by another part, often at a different pitch.

Imperfect cadence. At the end of a phrase, any chord – usually I, ii or IV – followed by a dominant chord (V).

Improvisation. The process of spontaneously creating new music as you perform.

Interrupted cadence. At the end of a phrase, a dominant chord followed by any other chord except for the tonic (usually VI).

Interval. The distance between two notes. For example, the interval between the notes F and A is a 3rd (A is the third note of the F major scale).

Jig. A traditional Irish dance in compound time.

Key. The key indicates the scale that a section or piece of music is based on. For example, music in the key of G major is mainly based around notes of the G major scale.

Largo. Italian for 'broad'. A slow tempo marking.

Lead singer. The principal singer e.g. in a jazz or pop band.

Leap. An interval greater than a tone.

Legato. Smooth playing, without gaps between the notes. May be indicated by slurs or phrase marks. Opposite of **staccato**.

Leitmotif. A recurring musical motif, used throughout a piece to illustrate the same person, emotion, place or something else.

Lieder. German for 'song'. Usually refers to songs with piano accompaniment written by Classical and Romantic German composers such as Schubert, Schumann and Brahms.

Looping/loop. Looping involves taking a short segment of music (a **loop**) and repeating it a number of times in succession.

Major and minor. Describe different types of intervals, chords, keys and scales. Minor intervals are smaller than major intervals by a semitone (for example F to A is a major third, whereas F to A♭ is a minor third). A major chord, key or scale contains a major third above the tonic, whereas a minor chord, scale or key contains a minor third (for example a D major chord contains the notes D, F♯ and A, while a D minor chord uses the notes D, F♮ and A).

Melisma. One syllable sung to several notes.

Metallophone. A tuned percussion instrument made up of metal bars, which are usually struck with a mallet.

Metronome mark. A metronome is a device that produces a regular number of clicks per minute, used to indicate the tempo or speed of a piece. A metronome marking tells us how fast to play a piece by specifying how many beats per minute there should be. For example, a metronome marking of ♩ = 60 means that there are 60 beats per minute, or one beat per second.

Middle eight. An eight-bar passage in the middle of a popular song, which contains contrasting music and prepares for the return of the main section.

MIDI (Musical Instrument Digital Interface). A music-industry standard format that allows electronic musical devices to link and communicate with each other, sharing information about features such as the length, pitch and dynamics of musical notes.

Minor. *See* **Major and minor**.

Mixing desk. A device that combines and controls audio signals from other equipment.

Moderato. Italian for 'moderate'. A medium tempo marking.

Modulation/modulate. Modulation is the process of changing key in a passage of music. When music **modulates** it changes from one key to another.

Monophonic. A texture that consists of only one melodic line.

Multi-tracking. A recording technique where different parts of a piece are recorded separately from one another and then mixed together to create the final recording.

Mute/muted. A **mute** is a device that can be fitted to an instrument to quieten its sound.

Notation. A score of a piece; music that has been written down using notes or other symbols.

Octave. An interval formed from two notes that are 12 semitones apart. Both notes have the same name.

Offbeat. An offbeat note is one that sounds in between the main beats of a piece of music.

Oral. To do with spoken or sung aspects of music; refers to using the mouth to speak, rather than the ear to hear.

Oratorio. A large choral work for vocal soloists, mixed choir and orchestra.

Ornament. A small musical addition that decorates a melody.

Orquesta tipica. A band that usually includes strings, bandoneón, piano and bass, and performs traditional tango music.

Ostinato. A repeating melodic, harmonic or rhythmic motif, heard continuously throughout part or the whole of a piece.

Overdubbing. Recording a new part over the top of existing material.

Overlay. *See* **Overdubbing**.

Panning. Panning is used in stereo recordings to control where the sound is coming from. Sounds can be panned to the left or right, or placed in the centre. For example, if a sound is panned left then it will be stronger in the left speaker.

Pélog. A seven-note scale used in gamelan music. It rises in unequal steps.

Perfect cadence. At the end of a phrase, a dominant chord (V) followed by a tonic chord (I).

Phrase. A short musical unit, similar to a phrase or a sentence in speech.

Phrasing. Refers to the **phrases** that make up a piece of music: how long they are and how they fit together.

Piano/pianissimo. A dynamic marking: quiet/very quiet.

Pitch. How high or low a note sounds. For example, in an ascending scale the pitch of the music rises, and notes lower down on the stave have a lower pitch.

Pizzicato. A direction to pluck notes on a string instrument.

Plagal cadence. At the end of a phrase, a subdominant chord (IV) followed by a tonic chord (I).

Polyphonic. A texture consisting of two or more equally important melodic lines heard together. The term has a similar meaning to **contrapuntal**, but is more often used for vocal rather than instrumental music.

Polyrhythm. Two distinct and contrasting rhythms that are played simultaneously.

Prégon and choro. Lead singer and chorus. In salsa music, the prégon (lead singer) commonly improvises short phrases that are answered by the choro (backing singers/chorus).

Presto. Italian for 'quickly'. A very fast tempo marking.

Pulse. A regularly recurring sense of beat common to most styles of music.

Quartet. A group of four players.

Question and answer. A pair of phrases in which the second one is heard as a reply to the first. Similar to **call and response**.

Raga. A type of scale used in Indian music.

Reel. A traditional Irish dance in simple time.

Relative major, relative minor. Keys that have the same key signature but a different tonic. The tonic of a relative minor is three semitones below the tonic of its relative major (for example C major and A minor, or F major and D minor).

Remix. A new version of an original song, which mixes up elements of the original recording and combines them with new material.

Retrograde motion. The pitches of a previously heard melody or rhythm presented in reverse order.

Reverb. Short for reverberation. Reverb is an effect used to alter music so that it sounds as if it was recorded in a reverberant, echoey space.

Riff. A short, catchy melodic or rhythmic idea that is repeated.

Ritenuto. Italian for 'hold back'. A tempo marking directing the performer to slow down.

Romantic. The period of music between 1830 and 1900.

Rondo. A musical structure in which a main melody alternates with contrasting sections (ABACADA).

Round. A song in which each part sings the same melody but starts at different times.

Rubato. Slight changes to the tempo of a performance – speeding up or slowing down to make the music more expressive.

Salsa. A type of popular dance developed in New York during the 1960s and 70s. It has Cuban, Puerto Rican and African influences, and incorporates elements of jazz, rock and pop.

Sample. A short section from a recorded audio track that can be digitally manipulated or altered for insertion into a new track.

Sampler. A device that stores, modifies and plays back recorded sounds known as samples.

Scale. A sequence of notes that move either upwards or downwards. Different types of scales have different patterns of intervals.

Scat. In jazz and blues music, the singing of nonsense syllables instead of words.

Scratching. A technique used in DJ-ing, which involves the DJ altering the playback speed of a disc by moving it backwards and forwards. This can give a very sudden and harsh sound, which gives the technique its name.

Semitone. Half of a tone. The smallest interval in Western music in general use. On the piano a semitone is the interval between any two keys, either black or white, which are right next to each other. For example, A–A♯, E–F or D♭–D.

Sequence. Immediate repetition of a melodic or harmonic idea at a different pitch, or a succession of different pitches.

Sequencer. An electronic device or piece of computer software that allows the user to create and edit **MIDI** and audio files.

Sitar. A plucked string instrument used to play the melody in Indian classical music.

Solo. A section or a piece of music that has a prominent part for one singer or instrumentalist, while the other musician(s) provide the accompaniment.

Son clave. A two-bar rhythmic pattern played by the claves in salsa music.

Sonero and choro. *See* **Prégon and choro**.

Soprano. The highest female voice.

Staccato. Detached. Refers to notes that are held for less time than their value indicates, so they are shortened and separated from each other. Indicated by a dot underneath or over a note. Opposite of **legato**.

Stab. Sharp, staccato chords.

Stave. The horizontal lines on and between which notes are written. The most common type of stave has five lines.

Step. An interval of a semitone or tone.

Strophic. A type of song in which the same music is used for each verse of the lyrics.

Subdominant. The fourth note of a scale. For example, D is the subdominant of A.

Swing rhythm. In jazz and the blues, a relaxing of strict quaver rhythm, so that ♪ ♪ is played as ♩♪ .

Syllabic. A song that has one note to each syllable.

Symphony. A type of orchestral composition, usually in four movements.

Syncopation. Placing the accents in parts of the bar that are not normally emphasised, such as on weak beats or between beats.

GLOSSARY

Synthesiser. An electronic device, usually controlled from a keyboard, that allows the player to create and manipulate electronic sounds.

Tabla. A pair of small, single-headed drums used in Indian classical music.

Tala. A cycle of beats that the tabla player improvises with in Indian classical music.

Tango. A type of popular dance that developed in Argentina during the late 19th century.

Tango nuevo. 'New tango'. A sub-genre of tango that developed during the 1980s, incorporating new elements (especially from jazz and classical music) into traditional tango.

Tanpura. A plucked string instrument used to play the drone in Indian classical music.

Tempo. The speed of the music. This is often indicated by a tempo marking at the beginning of a piece or passage of music.

Tenor. A high male voice.

Ternary. A musical structure of three sections. The outer sections are similar and the central one contrasting (ABA).

Texture. The number of layers of sound in a peice, and their relationship to each other. Three examples of types of texture are **homophonic**, **monophonic** and **polyphonic**.

Timbales. A pair of shallow, single-headed drums. Timbales originated in Cuba and are played in popular styles such as salsa.

Time signature. Two numbers (for example 2/4 or 6/8) at the start of a stave that indicate the metre of the music. The bottom number indicates the type of beat (such as crotchet or quaver) and the top number shows how many of those beats are in each bar.

Timpani. Also known as kettledrums, these are the large drums in the percussion section of an orchestra, each tuned to a different bass note.

Tone. An interval of two semitones, for example D–E and F♯–G♯.

Tonic. The starting note of a major or minor scale, and the note from which a key takes its name. For example, F is the tonic of F major and D the tonic of D minor.

Trance. A genre of electronic dance music that developed in the 1990s.

Transposing instrument. An instrument in which the sounding pitch differs from the written pitch of the instrument's part. For example, when a trumpet in B♭ plays a written C, it sounds as a B♭.

Treble. A voice with a similar range to a soprano, but normally referring to a child's voice, particularly that of a boy, rather than to the voice of an adult woman.

Tremolo. A musical effect that refers to a very quick repetition of a single note (e.g. on bowed or plucked string instruments) or of two alternating notes (e.g. on keyboard instruments).

Trill. An ornament (*tr*) consisting of a rapid alternation of two adjacent pitches.

Twelve bar blues. A standard chord sequence used in the blues and other popular music, which is based on the tonic (I), subdominant (IV) and dominant (V) chords of a key. Its most common form is I–I–I–I, IV–IV–I–I, V–IV–I–I.

Uilleann pipes. An Irish instrument similar to the Scottish bagpipes.

Unison. Simultaneous performance of the same pitch or pitches by more than one person.

Variation. A musical structure in which the main theme is varied a number of times (A, A1, A2).

Venue. The building or place in which a performance is held.

Verse. A section in a song with lyrics unique to that section: each verse in a song usually has the same music but different lyrics.

Vivace. Italian for 'lively'. A fast tempo marking.

Wah-wah. An effect that varies the timbre of sound, creating a speech-like 'wah wah' effect.

Walking bass. A bass line in which the notes are all on the beat, and move mainly by steps instead of leaps.

Waltz. A classical dance that first became popular in Austrian ballrooms during the 1770s. Usually in 3/4 with an um-cha-cha accompaniment.

Word painting. The use of musical devices and features to illustrate and highlight specific words in the lyrics.

Xylophone. A percussion instrument consisting of tuned wooden bars.

COPYRIGHT

Rhinegold Education is grateful to the following for permission to use printed excerpts from their publications:

One Day Like This. Garvey/Potter/Potter/Turner/Jupp. © 2008 Salvation Music Ltd (NS). All rights administered by Warner/Chappell Music Publishing Ltd. All Rights Reserved.

He's a Pirate. Words and Music by Klaus Badelt, Hans Zimmer and Geoffrey Zanelli. © 2004 Walt Disney Music (USA) Co, Warner/Chappell Artemis Music Ltd. Reproduced by permission of Faber Music Ltd. All Rights Reserved.

Gold and Silver Waltz – Franz Lehar. © Copyright 1904 by Glocken Verlag Ltd. Reproduced by permission of Boosey & Hawkes Music Publishers Ltd.

'Capsule in Space' (from *You Only Live Twice*). Music by John Barry. © 1967 United Artists Music Ltd. All rights controlled by EMI Unart Catalog Inc. (Publishing) and Alfred Music Publishing (Print). All Rights Reserved. Used by permission.

Where Eagles Dare. Music by Ron Goodwin. © 1968 Ole Grand Films, EMI Music Publishing Ltd. Reproduced by permission of International Music Publications Ltd (a trading name of Faber Music Ltd). All Rights Reserved.

'Berlin Foot Chase' (from *The Bourne Supremacy*). Music by John Powell. © Copyright 2004 Universal/MCA Music Ltd. All Rights Reserved. International Copyright Secured.

'A Call to Adventure' (Theme from *The Mummy 3*). Music by Randy Edelman. © Copyright 2008 Universal/MCA Music Ltd. All Rights Reserved. International Copyright Secured.

For An Angel. Words & Music by Paul Dyk Van & Johnny Klimek. © Universal Music Publishing MGB Ltd. All Rights Reserved. International Copyright Secured.

Hallelujah. Words & Music by Leonard Cohen. © Copyright 1984 Sony/ATV Music Publishing (UK) Ltd. All Rights Reserved. International Copyright Secured. Used by permission of Music Sales Ltd.